TOWN OF PELHAM PUBLIC LIBRARY

W9-BZO-809

DATE DUE

FEB 22 2005

I w
ian

I WANT TO BE A

Librarian

DAN LIEBMAN

FIREFLY BOOKS

A FIREFLY BOOK

Published by Firefly Books Ltd. 2003

First Printing 2003

Publisher Cataloging-in-Publication Data (U.S.)
(Library of Congress Standards)

Liebman, Dan.
   I want to be a librarian / Dan Liebman.—1st ed.
[24] p. : col. photos. ; cm.   –(I want to be)
Summary: Photographs and easy-to-read text describe the job of a librarian.
ISBN 1-55297-691-2
ISBN 1-55297-689-0 (pbk.)
1. Librarians – Vocational guidance 2. Occupations. I. Title. II. Series
331.124102 21   HD8039.L53.L54   2003

Published in the United States in 2003 by
Firefly Books (U.S.) Inc.
P.O. Box 1338, Ellicott Station
Buffalo, New York, USA, 14205

National Library of Canada Cataloguing in
Publication Data

Liebman, Daniel
   I want to be a Librarian

ISBN 1-55297-691-2 (bound)
ISBN 1-55297-689-0 (pbk.)

1. Librarians– Juvenile literature.   I. Title

Z682.L54 2003   j020'.23   C2002-903691-7

Published in Canada in 2003 by
Firefly Books Ltd.
3680 Victoria Park Avenue
Toronto, Ontario, Canada, M2H 3K1

Photo Credits

© AP Photo/Jacqueline Roggenbrodt, pages 10-11

© Harry Cutting Photography, page 9

© Chip Henderson/MaXx Images, front cover, page 18

© Mark E. Gibson Stock Photography, pages 6-7

© Monroe County Public Library; Bloomington, IN, page 23

© SW Productions/Getty Images, page 12

© George Walker/Firefly Books, pages 5, 8, 13, 14, 15, 16, 17, 19, 20-21, 22, 24, back cover

The author and publisher would like to thank:

Baycrest Centre for Geriatric Care, Toronto
Inta McCaughey, Bruce Public School, Toronto
Katherine Quan, Jones Public Library, Toronto
Saira Mall, Greg Patterson and
V.W. Bladen Library at University of Toronto at Scarborough
Debbie Johnson-Houston

Design by Interrobang Graphic Design Inc.
Printed and bound in Canada by Friesens, Altona, Manitoba

The Publisher acknowledges the financial support of the Government of Canada through the Book Publishing Industry Development Program for its publishing activities.

Welcome to the library! Librarians like working with books.

Librarians help people find the books they want.

This student is working on a project. The librarian has helped her find the right book.

Librarians choose the books for the library. These children like all the new books.

With a library card, you can borrow books.

Librarians help explain things to people.

The computer catalog helps people find what they're looking for.

Librarians or their helpers put materials back on the shelves. A helper is called a "page."

This girl likes animal stories. The librarian shows her an interesting book.

This librarian works in a hospital. She helps doctors and nurses find information.

This children's librarian is reading out loud. Every week there is a special storybook afternoon.

There are libraries in schools and colleges.

Sometimes, the library goes to the readers. A traveling library is called a "bookmobile."

Librarians have a busy job. But what could be better than sharing a book with other people?

We're from
Italy

Emma Lynch

Heinemann Library
Chicago, Illinois

Customer Service 888-454-2279
Visit our website at www.heinemannlibrary.com

Editorial: Jilly Attwood, Kate Bellamy, Adam Miller
Design: Ron Kamen, Celia Jones
Picture research: Maria Joannou, Erica Newbery
Photographer: Sharron Lovell
Production: Severine Ribierre

Originated by Ambassador Litho Ltd
Printed and bound in China by South China Printing Company Ltd

09 08 07 06
10 9 8 7 6 5 4 3 2

Library of Congress Cataloging-in-Publication Data
Lynch, Emma.
  We're from Italy / Emma Lynch.
    p. cm. -- (We're from ...)
  Includes bibliographical references and index.
  ISBN 1-4034-5805-7 (lib. binding-hardcover) -- ISBN 1-4034-5814-6 (pbk.) 1. Italy--Social life and customs--Juvenile literature. 2. Children--Italy--Juvenile literature. 3. Family--Italy--Juvenile literature. I. Title. II. Series: We're from.
  DG451.L96 2005
  945.093--dc22

                              2005002616

Acknowledgements
The publishers would like to thank the following for permission to reproduce photographs:
Corbis/Royalty Free p. **30c** ; Harcourt Education pp. **1, 5a, 5b, 5c, 6a, 6b, 7, 8, 9a, 9b, 10, 11, 12a, 12b, 13a, 13b, 14a, 14b, 15, 16, 17, 18, 19, 20a, 20b, 21a, 21b, 22a, 22b, 23, 24a, 24b, 25, 26a, 26b, 27, 28a, 28b, 29a, 29b, 30b** (Sharron Lovell); Photodisc p. **30a**.

Cover photograph of Alberto and his friend, reproduced with permission of Harcourt Education Ltd/Sharron Lovell.

Many thanks to Lucia, Sara, Alberto, and their families.

Contents

Some words are shown in bold, **like this**. You can find out what they mean by looking in the glossary.

Where Is Italy?

To learn more about Italy, we meet three children who live there. Italy is a country in Europe. Italy is surrounded by the Mediterranean Sea.

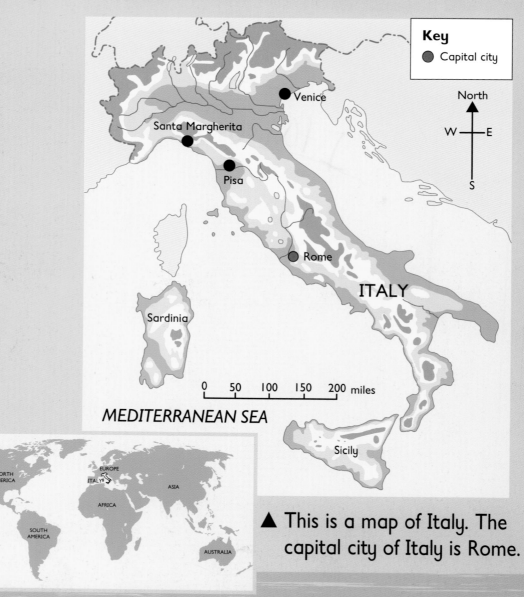

Key
- Capital city

North
W — E
S

Venice

Santa Margherita

Pisa

Rome

ITALY

Sardinia

0   50   100   150   200 miles

MEDITERRANEAN SEA

Sicily

NORTH AMERICA

EUROPE
ITALY

ASIA

AFRICA

SOUTH AMERICA

AUSTRALIA

▲ This is a map of Italy. The capital city of Italy is Rome.

Winters are very cold in northern Italy. Summers are very hot in southern Italy. There are **earthquakes** and **volcanoes** in some places in Italy.

Italy has hills and ▶ mountains. It also has flat, low land near the sea.

Meet Lucia

Lucia is six years old. She lives with her mother, father, sister, and brother. Her family live in an apartment in Rome, the capital city of Italy.

Lucia

Lucia's sister

▲ Lucia's father is an **architect**. Her mother is a teacher.

▼ Lucia likes eating spaghetti!

Lucia's mother

Lucia's father

Lucia's sister

Lucia

Lucia's family has a meal together in
the evening. Lucia helps by setting the
table. On special days they eat fish.
Lucia prefers eating cottage cheese or
ice cream.

7

Lucia's Day

Lucia goes to school five days a week. She studies math, Italian, art, music, religion, and English. Lucia likes art because it is messy!

Lucia's mother

Lucia walks to ► school with her mother.

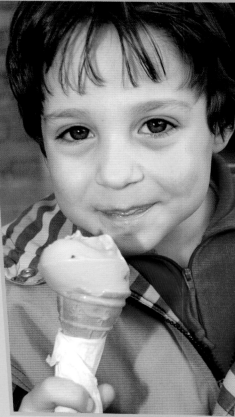

▲ For a treat,
Lucia is allowed
an ice cream cone!

After school, Lucia is taken care of by
her mother. Sometimes they go for a
walk around Rome. There are a lot of
interesting places to visit in Rome.

Playtime

When Lucia is not at school, she likes to play. She plays with her brother and sister. The apartment block she lives in has a big garden to play in.

◀ Lucia likes to go swimming and to ride her bike.

10

Lucia has lots of friends. She likes to play in the park with her friends. Her best friend is Adriana. She and Lucia tell each other jokes.

▼ Lucia likes funny friends who make her laugh.

Historic Buildings

Italy has a very interesting past. Many tourists visit Italy to see its **ancient** landmarks. The Colosseum in Rome was built by the ancient Romans nearly 2,000 years ago.

▼ People used to watch **gladiators** fight at the Colosseum.

People can walk to the top of the tower. ▶

The Leaning Tower of Pisa was built about 900 years ago. It took more than 200 years to finish. The tower was built straight but now it leans to one side!

13

Meet Sara

Sara is seven years old. She lives with her mother, father, and sister. Sara and her family live in Venice. Venice is made up of lots of small islands.

▼ There are lots of **canals** running through Venice.

▼ Sara's father has to work on weekends. Her family tries to spend time together when he is not working.

Sara's mother

Sara's father

Sara

Sara's sister

There are no cars or buses in Venice. People travel by boat. One boat used in Venice is called a **gondola**. Sara's father takes people around Venice in a gondola.

15

Fun in Venice

Sara goes to school five days a week. After school she plays with her sister and her friends. She likes to read books, skate, and ride her bike.

There are no ▶ cars in Venice so it is very safe to skate.

Sometimes Sara and her mother and sister visit her father on his **gondola**. He takes them for trips around the city.

▼ Sara's father wears a **traditional** uniform at work.

17

Chocolate!

Venice is famous for its pizza and seafood. Sara likes pizza, but she loves eating chocolate. She enjoys making sandwiches with chocolate spread!

▼ Sara's favorite food is chocolate spread!

Sara looks forward to special days and **festivals** in the year. Her favorite time is Easter. She and her sister receive lots of chocolate Easter eggs.

Making and Growing Things

People in Italy make and grow lots of goods to sell around the world. Venice is famous for its masks. People can watch them being made.

▶ One of the islands in Venice is called Murano. Murano is famous for the glass that is made there.

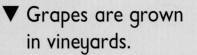 ▼ Grapes are grown in vineyards.

▲ Oranges grow well in southern Italy.

Different foods grow well in different parts of Italy. Wheat, grapes, olives, figs, and oranges all grow in Italy. There are also fields full of colorful sunflowers.

21

Meet Alberto

Alberto is eight years old. He lives with his mother, father, and sister in a small town called Santa Margherita. Santa Margherita is near the sea.

◀ Alberto lives a few minutes from the beach.

▼ Alberto's family always eats breakfast together at the weekend.

Alberto

Alberto's mother

Alberto's sister

Alberto's father

Alberto's parents work by helping people who visit Italy on vacation. His father has to work away from home all week. On weekends, the family likes to spend time together.

Alberto's School

Alberto goes to school five days a week. He studies math, Italian, English, art, music, and religion. He likes math and Italian. He really enjoys playing sports.

▼ There are 23 children in Alberto's class.

Alberto has many friends. He likes
talking to Enrico, and he plays soccer
with Lorenzo and Fredrico. His friend
Fabio makes him laugh a lot.

After School

After school, Alberto does his homework. When he has finished, he likes to play soccer with his friends in the park. Alberto loves playing outside.

▲ Alberto wants to be a soccer player when he is older.

▼ Alberto sometimes meets his grandmother when she walks her dog.

Alberto also enjoys swimming and playing the drums. His grandparents live nearby, so he sometimes sees them after school.

Food

Italy is known for its tasty food. The markets sell delicious tomatoes and olives. Pizza and pasta are Italian foods. Today, they are eaten all over the world!

▼ Pizzas are made in special pizza ovens.

28